iSucceed MATH™

DIAGNOSTIC PLACEMENT TESTS

Credits

Writing: Marlys Mahajan

Design/Production: Taurins Design

Electronic Art: Deborah Brouwer/Taurins Design

Cover and Package Design: Kristen Davis/Great Source

Editorial: Bob Cornell, Carol DeBold, Marc Hurwitz, Marianne Knowles, Marlys Mahajan

Contents

INTRODUCTION 2

GRADE 3 DIAGNOSTIC PLACEMENT TEST 4

GRADE 4 DIAGNOSTIC PLACEMENT TEST 9

GRADE 5 DIAGNOSTIC PLACEMENT TEST 16

GRADE 6 DIAGNOSTIC PLACEMENT TEST 24

GRADE 7/8 DIAGNOSTIC PLACEMENT TEST 32

USING THE DIAGNOSTIC PLACEMENT TEST RUBRICS 40

GRADE 3 ANSWER KEY 42

GRADE 4 ANSWER KEY 43

GRADE 5 ANSWER KEY 44

GRADE 6 ANSWER KEY 45

GRADE 7/8 ANSWER KEY 46

How to Use These Tests

Introduction

A student's personal math history is the best source of information about his or her mathematical understandings and skills. This personal history ideally includes classroom grades from previous years, standardized test scores, notes and recommendations from previous teachers, and samples of student work. Often, however, a student arrives in your classroom with few or none of these documents, yet you are expected to meet this child's needs as completely as those of a student with a long history of mathematical learning.

Why Diagnostic Placement Tests?

Using the *iSucceed MATH*™ Diagnostic Placement Tests will give you a base line for the mathematical understandings and skills of students for whom you have little or no history. An overall score for the test can help you decide whether a student needs intervention or not. The five Diagnostic Placement Tests correspond to grade levels and test content from earlier grades. For example, the Diagnostic Placement Test for grade 3 tests the skills and concepts normally taught in grades 1 and 2.

Structure of the Diagnostic Placement Tests

Each Diagnostic Placement Test is divided into sections corresponding to the volumes of *iSucceed MATH*™ applicable to your grade level. You can use a student's score in each section of the test to identify in which volume to start this student. After you select a curriculum for a given volume, the student takes an on-line pretest to identify the lessons that she or he needs to master.

Student History
- Test scores
- Teacher recommendations

and/or

Diagnostic Placement Test
- Objectives taken from earlier grades
- Guide to Volume selection

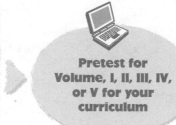

Pretest for Volume, I, II, III, IV, or V for your curriculum

For the Student: Lesson Menu
- List of courseware assignments to complete
- Assigned electronically

and

For the Teacher: Student Test Report
- List of courseware assignments for all students
- On-line pretest results

The pretest for your courseware curriculum gives you information about the strengths and weaknesses in your students' backgrounds. Thus *iSucceed MATH*™ allows each student to focus on a set of targeted objectives in weak areas rather than on familiar material. This targeted learning helps you to maximize student gains during the limited time that you have with your students each day.

Program Components for iSucceed MATH™

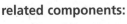

Program Overview
- Orientation to the program
- Implementation Plans
- Professional Papers
- Scope and Sequence

Guide for using the program

Teacher's Guide
- Concept-Builder and Skill-Builder lessons
- Active Practice model lessons

Whole- and small-group instruction

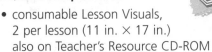

related components:
- consumable Lesson Visuals, 2 per lesson (11 in. × 17 in.) also on Teacher's Resource CD-ROM
- Vocabulary Cards
- Cardstock

Courseware
- Web-based lessons and assessments
- Practice Sheets and Family Activity Letters
- Student Lesson Reports and Lesson Support

Individualized instruction

related components:
- Diagnostic Placement Tests
- Practice Sheets and Family Activity Letters also on Teacher's Resource CD-ROM

Active Practice
- Math games on cards
- Models in Teacher's Guide

Small-group and paired practice

related components:
- number cubes
- Cardstock
- Active Practice Recording Sheets (in Teacher's Guide and on CD-ROM)

Tutoring Plans
- Lesson plan book

One-on-one remedial instruction

related components:
- *Math to Know*
- *Math at Hand*
- *Math on Call*
- Cardstock

Fact Fluency*
- Student Edition with flash cards
- Annotated Teacher's Edition

Active and independent practice for mastery

* Volume I only

Teacher's Resource CD-ROM
Resources for instruction and practice, to print out or to project on interactive whiteboards

Name:

Place Value and Basic Number Skills

1. 4 + 5 = _____

2. 6 + 8 = _____

3. 23 + 4 = _____

4. 5 + 14 = _____

5. 43 − 2 = _____

6. 18 − 10 = _____

Test Results

Items	Score	Find Help in Volume
1–19	/19	I
20–23	/4	II
24–28	/5	IV
29–30	/2	V

7. You have 12 baseball cards and your friend gives you 7 more. How many cards do you have now?

   _____ cards

8. You and your friend are writing a report together. You write 14 pages and your friend writes 12 pages. How many pages long is the report?

   _____ pages

9. You see 10 puppies in a room. Then 4 puppies go outside. How many are left?

   _____ puppies

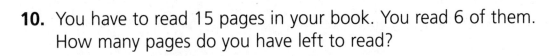

10. You have to read 15 pages in your book. You read 6 of them. How many pages do you have left to read?

_____ pages

11. A kitchen has 23 spoons, 14 forks and 12 knives. How many pieces of silverware are there in all?

_____ pieces of silverware

12. You have two baskets of oranges. One basket has 43 oranges and the other has 35 oranges. How many oranges do you have in all?

_____ oranges

13. $44 - 44 =$ _____

14. $27 + 0 =$ _____

15. $398 - 225 =$ _____

16. $67 - 52 =$ _____

17. $407 + 81 =$ _____

18. $12 + 13 + 14 =$ _____

19. A school has 479 students. There are 73 third graders. How many students are in the other grades?

_____ students

Decimals and Fractions

20. What is the value of the coins? _____ cents

21. How many dimes have the same value as 2 quarters?

_____ dimes

22. What is the value of the coins? _____ cents

23. How many nickels have the same value as 3 quarters and 2 dimes?

_____ nickels

Expressions and Equations

24. A bag has 24 toys in boxes. There are 6 balls, 8 tops, and 10 magic puzzles. You choose one box without looking. Which toy are you most likely to choose?

_____

25. You write the numbers 1 to 20 on slips of paper and put them in a hat. Your friend picks one slip without looking. Is the number more likely to be greater than 15 or less than 10?

_____

26. You toss a number cube. Is the number showing more likely to be an even number or a 5?

_____

27. Use the tally chart. How many people chose playing the piano or reading as their favorite hobby?

_____ people

Favorite Hobbies

Video games	ⵑ⵿⵿ ////
Playing piano	///
Reading	ⵑ⵿⵿ //

28. The tally chart shows what kinds of pets your friends have. Another friend says she has 6 fish. Show this answer in the tally chart.

Tally Chart of Pets

Name	Tally
Bird	//
Cat	////
Dog	//
Fish	

Measurement and Geometry

29. How long is the feather?

_____ centimeters

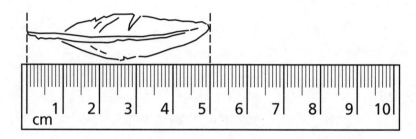

30. How tall is the plant?

_____ inches

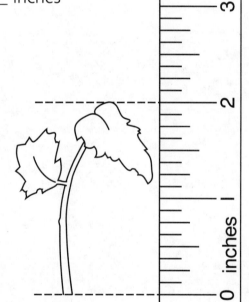

Name:

Place Value and Basic Number Skills

Test Results

Items	Score	Find Help in Volume
1–25	/25	I
26–30	/5	II
31–38	/8	IV
39–45	/6	V

1. What are the next 3 numbers in the pattern?

   490, 492, 494, 496, _____, _____, _____

2. What are the next 3 numbers in the pattern?

   125, 130, 135, 140, _____, _____, _____

3. What is the value of the digit 3 in the number 8,312?

   _____

4. What is the value of the digit 5 in the number 5,980?

   _____

5. What is the number 416 in expanded form?

   _____

6. What is $2,000 + 900 + 40 + 5$ in standard form?

   _____

7. Write the numbers in order from least to greatest.

   550   55   505   50

   _____

8. Write a number sentence that compares the values of 993 and 939.

   _____

9. Keshawn picks 48 apples at an apple orchard. His sister Maya picks 39 apples. How many apples do they pick in all?

    _____ apples

10. $45 + 27 + 36 + 12 = $ _____

11. Mr. Mack has a pack of 75 marking pens for the art club. He orders a new pack with 144 marking pens. How many marking pens does he have in all?

    _____ marking pens

12. $446 + 458 = $ _____

13. Louise has 33 nickels. Then she spends 5 of them. How many nickels does she have left?

    _____ nickels

14. $428 - 76 = $ _____

15. $907 - 368 = $ _____

16. The James School has 107 students. The Cutler School has 78 students. How many more students are in the James School?

    _____ more students

17. $4 \times 8 = $ _____

18. At Adams School each of the 4 classes of fourth graders has 27 students. How many fourth grade students does the school have?

    _____ students

19. Sophia planted her flower garden in this arrangement.

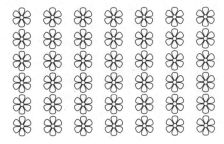

How many flowers did Sophia plant?

_____ flowers

20. Juice boxes are sold in packages that have 3 boxes. Troy buys 6 packages. How many juice boxes is this?

_____ juice boxes

21. $9 \times 418 =$ _____ .

22. $5 \times 5,076 =$ _____

23. What division sentence is in the same fact family as $6 \times 8 = 48$?

_____

24. $56 \div 8 =$ _____

25. Kyle has 36 colored pencils in 4 boxes. All the boxes have the same number of pencils. How many pencils are in each box?

_____ pencils

Decimals and Fractions

26. What is the value of the money shown? _____

27. What fraction of the model is shaded? _____

28. Patrick cuts a tray of lasagna into 10 equal pieces. His family eats $\frac{7}{10}$ of the lasagna for dinner. What fraction of the lasagna is left? _____

29. Write a fraction addition sentence for the shaded areas of this model.

_____

30. Write a fraction subtraction sentence for the shaded areas of this model.

_____

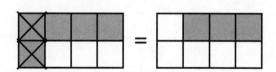

Expressions and Equations

31. Draw the next two figures in this pattern.

        _____ _____

32. What are the next two numbers in this pattern?

3, 7, 11, 15, _____, _____, _____

33. Mohan has a bag of 40 marbles. He has pulled out 22 marbles so far and is making a graph of his results.

How many units tall should Mohan make the bar for Red?

_____ squares tall

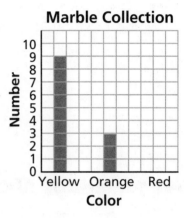

Marble Collection

34. Two adults are taking a child to a movie. The cost of children's tickets is $5, and the cost of an adult ticket is $8. What number expression shows how much the 3 tickets cost?

_____

35. Crystal has 9 pencils. Gwen gives her half of her 16 pencils. What number expression shows how many pencils Crystal has now?

_____

36. You have a bag that has 4 red counters, 5 green counters, and 10 blue counters. You draw one counter out of the bag without looking. What color is it most likely to be?

_____

37. You have a box full of marbles. How likely are you to draw a cat out of this box: certain, maybe, or impossible?

_____

38. You have a bag of pattern blocks. You pulled out 22 blocks: 6 squares, 7 rectangles, and 9 triangles. You want to show your results on a bar graph.

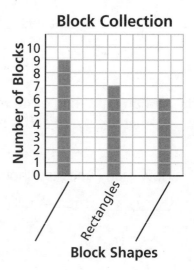

What labels should you write for the other two bars?

First bar: _____

Third bar: _____

Measurement and Geometry

Write the time shown on the clock.

39. _____

40. _____

41. What temperature does the thermometer show?

_____

42. Write the temperatures from coldest to warmest.

_____

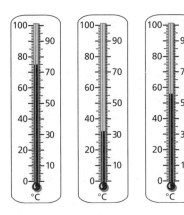

43. How many lines of symmetry does the triangle have? _____

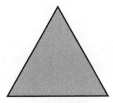

44. What shape is the front of this pattern block?

_____

45. Which of the dashed lines are lines of symmetry of the quilt square?

_____

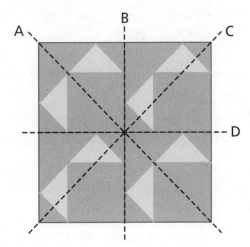

Name:

Place Value and Basic Number Skills

Items	Score	Find Help in Volume
1–15	/15	I
16–31	/16	II
32–36	/5	IV
37–46	/10	V

1. Write ten thousand, six hundred fifty-nine in standard form.

   _____

2. Write 519,206 in expanded form.

   _____

3. A movie theater sold 2,256,709 tickets one summer. What is this number rounded to the nearest thousand?

   _____

4. Estimate the sum 9,562 + 6,819 to the nearest thousand.

   _____

5. $4,567 - 2,761 =$ _____

6. $2,543 + 7,477 =$ _____

7. The three middle schools in Brewster school district have 495 students, 527 students, and 462 students. How many middle school students does the district have?

   _____

8. Two homes on Park Street are selling for $256,900 and $312,000. What is the difference in the cost of the two homes?

   _____

9. 72 × 66 = _____

10. 4,057 × 58 = _____

11. 8,154 ÷ 9 = _____

12. 2,598 ÷ 12 = _____

13. A carton of AA batteries contains 218 packages. Each package has 8 batteries. How many batteries are in a full carton?

_____

14. A jetliner has seats for 360 passengers. Each row has 8 seats. How many rows are there?

_____

15. The students at Edmont School are going by bus on a field trip. Each bus can carry 28 students. How many buses are needed to carry the 375 students?

_____

Decimals and Fractions

16. José buys 5 apples at the store. Each one costs $1.35. How much do the 5 apples cost?

_____

17. Rosa has $10 to spend at the mall. She buys 4 hair clips that cost $1.55 each. How much money does she have left to spend?

_____

18. The Robinsons have a daily newspaper delivered to their home. The cost is $7.20 each week. How much does it cost to have the paper delivered for 12 weeks?

_____

19. What is nine and seventeen hundredths in standard form?

_____

20. What is the expanded form of 15.27?

_____

21. Write a number sentence that compares 9.7 and 9.07.

_____

22. $3.14 + 7.2 + 0.119 =$ _____

23. $8.7 - 6.25 =$ _____

24. The table shows the distances between four towns. How many miles is the route from Shawsheen to Lovett to Campbell to Edwina?

_____

Towns	Distance
Shawsheen and Lovett	16.8 miles
Lovett and Campbell	15.4 miles
Campbell and Edwina	9.6 miles

25. Write two fractions that are equivalent to $\frac{4}{5}$. _____

26. Write a number sentence that compares the fractions $\frac{4}{10}$ and $\frac{10}{25}$.

_____

27. What mixed number is shown on the number line? _____

28. $\frac{2}{9} + \frac{4}{9} =$ _____

29. $\frac{7}{8} - \frac{5}{8} =$ _____

30. Martin gives $\frac{1}{10}$ of his allowance to charities, saves $\frac{2}{10}$ of it, and spends the rest of it. What fraction of his allowance does he spend?

_____

31. At the deli counter Kayla buys $1\frac{3}{8}$ pounds of sliced turkey and $\frac{7}{8}$ pound of sliced ham. How much more turkey than ham does she buy?

_____

Expressions and Equations

Use the bar graph to answer items 32 and 33. The graph shows the kinds of pets that the fifth grade students in one school have.

Pets Owned by Students

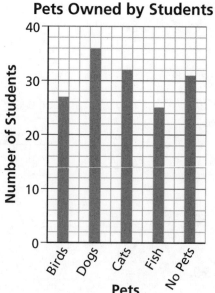

32. Which pet do 25 students have?

_____

33. What is the total number of pets owned by the students?

_____

Use the picture graph for items 34–36. The graph shows the number of hours of television that five friends watched in two weeks.

34. Who watched the most TV?

_____

35. How many hours of television did Robert watch?

_____

36. How many more hours of television did Sonya watch than Sophia?

_____

Time Spent Watching TV

Jamal			
Robert			
Sheila			
Sonya			
Sophia			

Key: = 12 hours

Measurement and Geometry

37. In one year February 1 is on a Tuesday. On what day of the week is February 15?

_____

38. Jerome visits his grandmother during the summer. He arrives on June 15 and leaves on July 10. How long was his visit?

_____

39. You want to measure the length of a basketball court. Would you measure the length in inches, yards, or miles?

_____

40. Is your height closer to 1.3 millimeters, 1.3 centimeters, 1.3 meters, or 1.3 kilometers?

_____

41. Is the capacity of a large drinking glass closer to 350 milliliters, 350 liters, or 350 kiloliters?

_____

42. The length of each side of a square is 27 inches. What is the perimeter of the square?

_____

43. What is the perimeter of the triangle?

_____

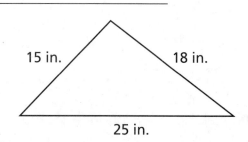

44. The length of a rectangle is 5 feet and its
width is 3 feet. What is the area of the rectangle?

_____

45. What is the area of the figure in square units?

_____

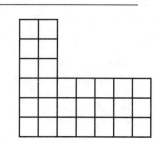

46. Andrea moved triangle A to form triangle B. Did Andrea use a slide,
a flip or a turn?

_____

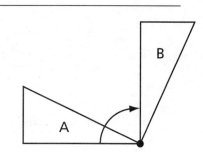

Name: _____

Place Value and Basic Number Skills

Test Results

Items	Score	Find Help in Volume
1–15		/15 I
16–33		/18 II
34–36		/3 III
37–44		/8 IV
45–59		/15 V

1. $5,635 - 287 =$ _____

2. $187,256 + 366,051 + 380,234 =$ _____

3. $5,852 \div 38 =$ _____

4. $25,760 \times 38 =$ _____

5. $589 \times 406 =$ _____

6. A company made 3,700 boxes of cereal and packed them into shipping cartons. Each carton contained 24 boxes. How many full cartons were packed?

_____

7. What are the prime factors of 42? _____

8. List all the composite numbers greater than 30 and less than 40.

_____

9. Write 345 as the product of prime factors.

_____

10. List all the whole numbers less than 20 that are factors of 750.

_____

Name: _____

11. The number 3■2 is evenly divisible by 9. What digit does ■ represent?

_____

12. What is the least number that can be evenly divided by 2, 3, 4, and 5?

_____

13. $6 \times 8 - (25 \div 5) =$ _____

14. $(102 \div 6) + 19 =$ _____

15. $(22 - 4) \times 2 \div 9 =$ _____

Decimals, Fractions, and Other Rational Numbers

16. What is seventy-seven and eighty-two thousandths in standard form?

_____

17. Gas station A is selling gasoline for $3.339 per gallon. Gas station B is selling it for $3.299 per gallon. How much more expensive is gasoline at station A than at station B?

_____

18. Round 96.052 to the nearest tenth. _____

19. $3.154 + 4.87 =$ _____

20. $4.3 - 2.049 =$ _____

21. Write two fractions that are equivalent to $\frac{2}{5}$. _____

Name: _____

22. What fraction does the model represent?

Write your answer in simplest form. _____

23. What is $\frac{16}{24}$ in simplest form? _____

24. What mixed number does the model show? _____

  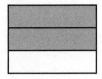

25. What is $1\frac{5}{8}$ written in fraction form? _____

26. You are making a sandbox for your younger brother. You need $3\frac{1}{3}$ feet of lumber for each of the 4 sides. How many feet of lumber do you need for this project?

_____

27. $1\frac{4}{9} - \frac{7}{9} =$ _____

28. What is $\frac{1}{3}$ of 36? _____

29. Leslie has 24 books. She gave $\frac{3}{8}$ of them to her friend. How many books did she give?

_____ books

30. Write a number sentence that compares 88 and −90.

_____

31. What temperature does the thermometer show? _____

32. Which point is at -7 on the number line? _____

33. Use the number line. Plot and label point A at $1\frac{1}{2}$ and point B at $-\frac{1}{2}$.

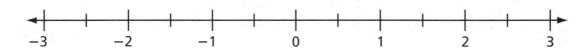

Ratios, Rates, and Percents

34. Write $\frac{9}{10}$ as a decimal and a percent.

Decimal: _____

Percent: _____

35. Baseball caps are on sale: 2 caps for $5. Complete the table to show the cost for different numbers of caps.

Number of caps	2	4	6	8	10
Cost (dollars)	5				

36. Write a fraction, decimal, and percent to represent the shaded portion of the square.

Fraction: _____

Decimal: _____

Percent: _____

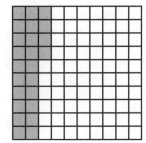

Expressions and Equations

37. How many squares should be in the eighth figure of the pattern below?

_____ squares

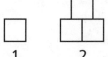

| 1 | 2 | 3 | 4 |

Figure Number

38. Write a number sentence for the following: The product of 8 and the sum of n and 13 is 144.

_____

39. The width of a rectangle is 21 cm and its length is w cm. Write an expression for the perimeter of the rectangle.

_____

40. The formula $F = (C \times 1.8) + 32$ is used to convert degrees Celsius to degrees Fahrenheit. Use the formula to find F when $C = 15$

_____

Use the graph for items 41 and 42.

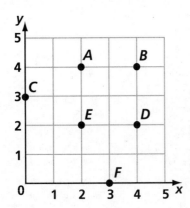

41. Which point on the coordinate grid locates the ordered pair (2, 4)?

_____

42. Which point on the coordinate grid locates the ordered pair (3, 0)?

_____

43. Sam is a member of a 10-person team. Each day one player on the team is chosen at random to lead the warm-ups for that day. What is the probability that Sam will be chosen to lead the players on Monday?

_____

44. What is the probability of spinning a 2 using the spinner? Write the probability as a fraction, decimal and percent.

Fraction: _____

Decimal: _____

Percent: _____

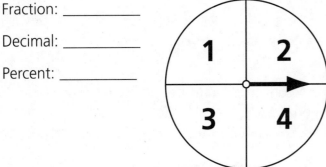

Name: _____

Measurement and Geometry

45. A movie starts at 5:20 P.M. and lasts until 7:10 P.M. How long is the movie?

_____ hours _____ minutes

46. You go canoeing with your friends one Saturday. You leave home at 8:40 A.M. and return at 5:25 P.M. How long were you gone?

_____ hours _____ minutes

47. On Sunday the train to Milwaukee leaves at 10:42 A.M. The next train leaves 18 hours 45 minutes later. What time on Monday does it leave?

_____

For items 48–51 write the equivalent measurement.

48. 3 yards = _____ feet

49. 500 cm = _____ meters

50. 8 pounds = _____ ounces

51. 0.5 kilogram = _____ grams

52. How many sides does an octagon have? _____

53. What is the name of this figure? _____

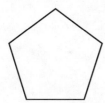

54. A triangle has two angles that each measure 50°.

What is the measure of the third angle?

_____

55. What is the measure of angle *W*? _____

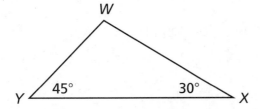

Use the figure below for items 56–59.

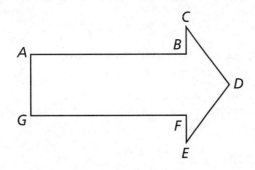

56. Name an obtuse angle. _____

57. Name an acute angle. _____

58. Name a line segment that appears parallel to segment *GF*.

_____

59. Name a line segment that appears perpendicular to segment *GF*.

_____

Name: _____

Place Value and Basic Number Skills

1. $55 \times 87 =$ _____

2. $5{,}296 \div 44 =$ _____

3. $128 \times 302 =$ _____

4. $58{,}800 \div 336 =$ _____

5. $7 \times 12 - 24 \div 6 =$ _____

6. $4 \times 16 - 2 \times (25 - 18) =$ _____

7. What is the greatest common factor of 12 and 18? _____

8. What is the least common multiple of 6 and 8? _____

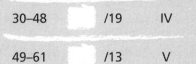

Test Results

Items	Score	Find Help in Volume
1–8	/8	I
9–18	/10	II
19–29	/11	III
30–48	/19	IV
49–61	/13	V

Decimals, Fractions, and Other Rational Numbers

9. A scientist has 5.4 milliliters of a liquid that is 8% water. How many milliliters of water are in the liquid?

_____

10. $24.8 \div 1.6 =$ _____

11. Order the fractions from least to greatest: $\frac{3}{4}, \frac{3}{8}, \frac{3}{5}$.

_____

12. The lengths of three roses are $2\frac{3}{4}$ feet, $2\frac{5}{6}$ feet and $2\frac{2}{3}$ feet. Write the lengths from shortest to longest.

_____

13. $1\frac{3}{4} + 2\frac{3}{8} =$ _____

14. $\frac{5}{8} \times \frac{4}{25} =$ _____

15. You have $3\frac{1}{3}$ cups of rice. You use $1\frac{1}{2}$ cups for dinner. How many cups of rice are left?

_____

16. You want to fill a gap of $7\frac{1}{3}$ minutes in a talent show by playing a recording that is $2\frac{14}{15}$ minutes long. How many times should you play the recording?

_____

17. Write "a loss of 15 yards" as an integer. _____

18. Write "a deposit of $25 followed by a withdrawal of $10" as the sum of two integers.

_____

Ratios, Rates, and Percents

19. Write the ratio of turtles to fish in three ways.

_____

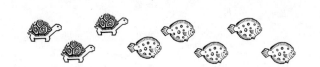

In items 20–22, write the ratio of hits to at-bats as a fraction, decimal, and percent.

Roberto has 6 hits in 25 at-bats so far this season.

20. Fraction: _____   **21.** Decimal: _____   **22.** Percent: _____

23. A company spent $62 to buy 40 metal straps. How much did it pay per strap?

_____

24. You travel 162 miles in 3 hours. At the same speed, how far can you travel in 5 hours?

_____

25. On a map, $\frac{5}{8}$ inch represents 40 miles. What distance does $4\frac{1}{2}$ inches represent?

_____

26. Write $\frac{9}{10}$ as a percent. _____

27. Write 12% as a decimal. _____

28. What is 45% of 220? _____

29. A survey asks 200 students what their favorite type of music is. Rock music was chosen by 37% of the students. How many students chose Rock as their favorite type of music?

_____

Expressions and Equations

30. What property of addition does the number sentence show?
$a + (7 + b) = a + (b + 7)$

_____

31. What number property does the number sentence show?
$(2 \times a) + (2 \times b) = 2 \times (a + b)$

_____

For items 32 and 33, simplify the expression.

32. $3a + 7 + 6a = $ _____

33. $\dfrac{8a - 12b}{4} = $ _____

34. What is the value of $y + 13 - 2y + 5$ when $y = 8$?

_____

35. What is the value of $2a + \frac{1}{3} + a - \frac{7}{6}$ when $a = \frac{2}{3}$?

_____

36. What value of x makes the equation $2x + 3 = 5x$ true?

_____

37. Ana earns m dollars per hour for babysitting. The equation $5m = 30$ represents her pay for one 5-hour job. Solve the equation for m to find how much she earns each hour.

$m = $ _____

38. Complete the table of values. Use the rule $y = 4x + 5$.

x	0	1	2	3	4
y	5				

For items 39–41, use the data below. It shows the ages of ten people at a family gathering.

1   3   3   23   23   25   27   49   51   73

39. What is the range of the data? _____

40. What is the mean of the data? _____

41. What is the median of the data? _____

42. List all possible outcomes when spinning both spinners at the same time.

_____

 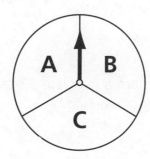

43. You toss a coin and roll a number cube, numbered from 1 to 6. What are the possible outcomes of this experiment? (Use H for heads and T for tails.)

_____

For items 44–46, use the line graph below. It shows the distance you traveled on a one-day bike trip.

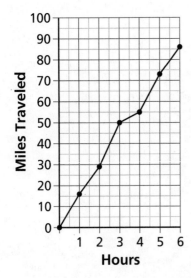

44. How many miles did you travel after the first three hours?

_____

45. During which hour of the trip did you travel the fewest miles? _____

46. How many miles did you travel in all? _____

47. The probability of drawing a red king from a standard 52-card deck is $\frac{1}{26}$. What is the probability of NOT drawing a red king?

_____

48. A bag contains the names of 8 people, including Bobby Joe and Allan. Two names are drawn without looking. What is the probability that Bobby Joe is drawn first and Allan is drawn second?

_____

Measurement and Geometry

For items 49 and 50, convert each measurement to the given unit.

49. $3\frac{1}{2}$ yards = _____ feet

50. 420 centimeters = _____ meters

For items 51–53, use the diagram below.

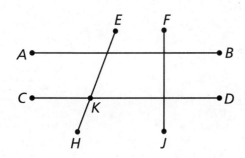

51. Name two line segments that seem to be perpendicular.

Segments _____ and _____

52. Name two line segments that seem to be parallel.

Segments _____ and _____

53. Name two angles, with vertex *K*, that are acute.

_____ and _____

For items 54 and 55, use the triangle below.

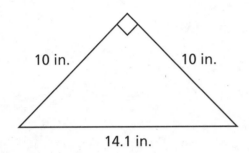

54. Classify the triangle as equilateral, isosceles, or scalene. _____

55. Classify the triangle as acute, obtuse, or right. _____

For items 56 and 57, use parallelogram *PQRS*.

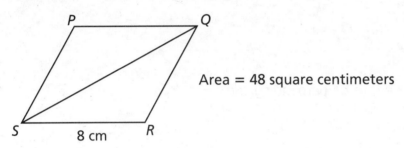

Area = 48 square centimeters

56. What is the height of parallelogram *PQRS*? _____

57. What is the area of triangle *QRS*? _____

58. What is the circumference of the circle? Use $\pi \approx 3\frac{1}{7}$.

_____

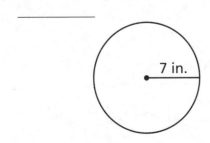

59. The two triangles are similar. Find the length of segment *AB*. _____

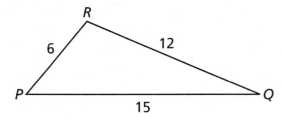 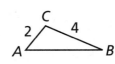

60. What is the volume of the prism? _____

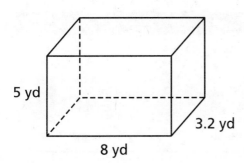

61. The area of each base of the prism is 15 square meters. What is its volume?

_____

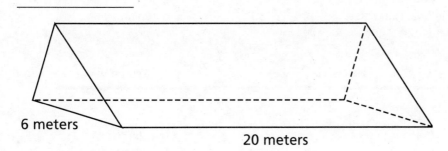

Using the Diagnostic Placement Test Rubrics

The five Diagnostic Placement Tests correspond to grade levels and test content normally taught in earlier grades. For example, the Diagnostic Placement Test for grade 3 tests the skills and concepts normally taught in grades 1 and 2. An overall score for the test can help you decide whether a students needs intervention or not, if, for example, the student is new to your district and information about student achievement is unavailable.

Each of the Diagnostic Placement Tests is divided into sections corresponding to the volumes of *iSucceed MATH*™ applicable to your grade level. You can use a student's score in each section and the rubrics below to identify in which volume to start this student. The courseware pretest for your curriculum will electronically assign an individualized set of lessons for the student to complete in this volume.

GRADE 3 PLACEMENT RUBRIC

Skill Area	Items	Remediate with. . .
Place Value and Basic Number Skills	1–19	Volume I
Decimals, Fractions, and Other Rational Numbers	20–23	Volume II
Expressions and Equations	24–28	Volume IV
Measurement and Geometry	29–30	Volume V

GRADE 4 PLACEMENT RUBRIC

Skill Area	Items	Remediate with. . .
Place Value and Basic Number Skills	1–25	Volume I
Decimals, Fractions, and Other Rational Numbers	26–30	Volume II
Expressions and Equations	31–38	Volume IV
Measurement and Geometry	39–45	Volume V

GRADE 5 PLACEMENT RUBRIC

Skill Area	Items	Remediate with. . .
Place Value and Basic Number Skills	1–15	Volume I
Decimals, Fractions, and Other Rational Numbers	16–31	Volume II
Expressions and Equations	32–36	Volume IV
Measurement and Geometry	37–46	Volume V

GRADE 6 PLACEMENT RUBRIC

Skill Area	Items	Remediate with. . .
Place Value and Basic Number Skills	1–15	Volume I
Decimals, Fractions, and Other Rational Numbers	16–33	Volume II
Ratios, Rates, and Percents	34–36	Volume III
Expressions and Equations	37–44	Volume IV
Measurement and Geometry	45–59	Volume V

GRADE 7/8 PLACEMENT RUBRIC

Skill Area	Items	Remediate with. . .
Place Value and Basic Number Skills	1–8	Volume I
Decimals, Fractions, and Other Rational Numbers	9–18	Volume II
Ratios, Rates, and Percents	19–29	Volume III
Expressions and Equations	30–48	Volume IV
Measurement and Geometry	49–61	Volume V

Place Value and Basic Number Skills

1. 9
2. 14
3. 27
4. 19
5. 41
6. 8
7. 19
8. 26
9. 6
10. 9
11. 49
12. 78
13. 0
14. 27
15. 173
16. 15
17. 488
18. 39
19. 406

Decimals and Fractions

20. 48
21. 5
22. 81
23. 19

Expressions and Equations

24. magic puzzle
25. less than 10
26. even number
27. 10
28. The tally for Fish should show: ~~||||~~ |

Measurement and Geometry

29. 5 cm
30. 2 in.

Place Value and Basic Number Skills

1. 498, 500, 502
2. 145, 150, 155
3. 300
4. 5,000
5. $4 \times 100 + 1 \times 10 + 6$
6. 2,945
7. 50, 55, 505, 550
8. $939 < 993$ or $993 > 939$
9. 87
10. 120
11. 219
12. 904
13. 28
14. 352
15. 539
16. 29
17. 32
18. 108
19. 42
20. 18
21. 3,762
22. 25,380
23. $48 \div 6 = 8$ or $48 \div 8 = 6$
24. 7
25. 9

Decimals and Fractions

26. $1.43
27. $\frac{4}{5}$
28. $\frac{3}{10}$
29. $\frac{1}{6} + \frac{2}{6} = \frac{3}{6}$ or $\frac{1}{6} + \frac{2}{6} = \frac{1}{2}$
30. $\frac{5}{8} - \frac{2}{8} = \frac{3}{8}$

Expressions and Equations

31. △ ▮
32. 19, 23, 27
33. 10
34. $5 + (2 \times 8)$ or $(2 \times 8) + 5$
35. $9 + (16 \div 2)$ or $(16 \div 2) + 9$
36. blue
37. impossible
38. First bar: Triangles
Third bar: Squares

Measurement and Geometry

39. 1:25
40. 4:42
41. 88°F
42. 32°C, 55°C, 75°C
43. 3
44. square
45. Line A

Place Value and Basic Number Skills

1. 10,659

2. $5 \times 100,00 + 1 \times 10,000 + 9 \times 1,000 + 2 \times 100 + 6$

3. 2,257,000

4. 17,000

5. 1,806

6. 10,020

7. 1,484

8. $55,100

9. 4,752

10. 235,306

11. 906

12. 216 R 6 or $216\frac{1}{2}$

13. 1,744

14. 45

15. 14

Decimals and Fractions

16. $6.75

17. $3.80

18. $86.40

19. 9.17

20. $1 \times 10 + 5 \times 1 + 2 \times \frac{1}{10} + 7 \times \frac{1}{100}$

21. $9.7 > 9.07$ or $9.07 < 9.7$

22. 10.459

23. 2.45

24. 41.8 miles

25. Answers may vary. Sample: $\frac{8}{10}$ and $\frac{20}{25}$

26. $\frac{4}{10} = \frac{10}{25}$

27. $1\frac{6}{8}$ or $1\frac{3}{4}$

28. $\frac{6}{9}$ or $\frac{2}{3}$

29. $\frac{2}{8}$ or $\frac{1}{4}$

30. $\frac{7}{10}$

31. $\frac{4}{8}, \frac{2}{4}$ or $\frac{1}{2}$

Expressions and Equations

32. fish

33. 120

34. Sonya

35. 30 hours

36. 18 hours

Measurement and Geometry

37. Tuesday

38. 25 days

39. yards

40. 1.3 meters

41. 350 milliliters

42. 108 inches

43. 58 inches

44. 15 square feet

45. 27 square units

46. a turn

Place Value and Basic Number Skills

1. 5,348
2. 933,541
3. 154
4. 978,880
5. 239,134
6. 154
7. 2, 3, and 7
8. 32, 33, 34, 35, 36, 38 and 39
9. $3 \times 5 \times 23$
10. 1, 2, 3, 5, 6, 10, and 15
11. 4
12. 60
13. 43
14. 36
15. 4

Decimals, Fractions, and Other Rational Numbers

16. 77.082
17. $.04
18. 96.1
19. 8.024
20. 2.251
21. Answers may vary. Sample $\frac{4}{10}$, $\frac{8}{20}$
22. $\frac{6}{8}$ or $\frac{3}{4}$
23. $\frac{2}{3}$
24. $2\frac{2}{3}$
25. $\frac{13}{8}$
26. $13\frac{1}{3}$ feet
27. $\frac{6}{9}$ or $\frac{2}{3}$
28. 12
29. 9
30. $-90 < 88$ or $88 > -90$

31. $-5°F$
32. B
33.

Ratios, Rates and Percents

34. 0.90 , 90%
35. 10, 15, 20, 25
36. $\frac{24}{100}$, 0.24, 24%

Expressions and Equations

37. 15
38. $8 \times (n + 13) = 144$
39. $42 + 2 \times w$ or $2 \times w + 42$
40. 59°F
41. A
42. F
43. 10%, or $\frac{1}{10}$ or 0.1
44. $\frac{1}{4}$, 0.25, 25%

Measurement and Geometry

45. 1 hr 50 min
46. 8 hr 45 min
47. 5:27 A.M
48. 9
49. 5
50. 128
51. 500
52. 8
53. pentagon
54. 80°
55. 105°
56. $\angle D$
57. $\angle BCD$ or $\angle DEF$
58. segment AB
59. segments FE, AG, or CB

Place Value and Basic Number Skills

1. 4,785
2. 120 R 16 or $120\frac{4}{11}$
3. 38,656
4. 175
5. 80
6. 50
7. 6
8. 24

Decimals, Fractions, and Other Rational Numbers

9. 0.432
10. 15.5
11. $\frac{3}{8}, \frac{3}{5}, \frac{3}{4}$
12. $2\frac{2}{3}$ feet, $2\frac{3}{4}$ feet, $2\frac{5}{6}$ feet
13. $4\frac{1}{8}$
14. $\frac{1}{10}$
15. $1\frac{5}{6}$ cups
16. $2\frac{1}{2}$
17. -15
18. $25 + (-10)$

Ratios, Rates, and Percents

19. $\frac{3}{5}$, 3 : 5, 3 to 5
20. $\frac{6}{25}$
21. 0.24
22. 24%
23. $1.55
24. 270 miles
25. 288 miles
26. 90%
27. 0.12
28. 99
29. 74

Expressions and Equations

30. Commutative property
31. Distributive property
32. $9a + 7$ or $7 + 9a$
33. $2a - 3b$
34. 10
35. $1\frac{1}{6}$ or $\frac{7}{6}$
36. 1
37. $6
38. 9, 13, 17, 21
39. 72 years
40. 27.8 years
41. 24 years
42. 2A, 2B, 2C, 4A, 4B, 4C, 6A, 6B, 6C
43. H-1, H-2, H-3, H-4, H-5, H-6, T-1, T-2, T-3, T-4, T-5, T-6
44. 50 miles
45. hour 4, or between 3 and 4
46. 86 miles
47. $\frac{25}{26}$
48. $\frac{1}{56}$

Measurement and Geometry

49. $10\frac{1}{2}$
50. 4.2
51. *AB* and *FJ* or *CD* and *FJ*
52. *AB* and *CD*
53. $\angle EKD$ and $\angle HKC$
54. isosceles
55. right
56. 6 cm
57. 24 cm²
58. about 44 in.
59. 5
60. 128 yd³
61. 300 m³